Expectations

(Book two)

Story of Tom and Abdullah

m. r. abdullah

copyright - 2020

Page 2

A brief summary from book one (Dreams)

Mary felt calm and happy. Soon she will become a muslim and also Abdullah's wife. 'thank you Malcolm-x and thank you very much God.' Mary said to herself. She ran upstairs to check on her son Adam. He is still sleeping but will be getting up soon for milk. 'soon my son will have a proper good daddy and I will get a good husband. I need to tell Tom about this so there is no complications between Abdullah, Tom and me. I will call him later or may be tomorrow.'

Chapter 1

Time now 7: 55pm, almost 8 pm. Mary sat down on her sofa really happy with a second cup of coffee watching East Enders. She still can't believe Abdullah loves her back infact Abdullah is and has been in love with her for a long time. As the clock past 8pm. She reminded herself to get a copy of the Quran, an english translation from the muslim centre on Yorkshire street because Malcolm X became muslim so there is something about islam that she needs to find out and she is hoping by reading the Quran she will get her answers.

Page 4

Mary lost in thought did not hear the knock on the front door. Then her mobile buzzed as it is infront of her she picked it up and saw the screen, Tom calling. She answered the phone and Tom said, "Hi mary are you not at home?"

'I'm at home Tom, what's up?" she does not hate Tom anymore. What has happened probably for the best.

"Oh that's great please open the door I am outside your front door." Said Tom and hung up. Mary ran to the door and opened it instantly.

"I am sorry Tom I did not hear the knock, so sorry. How are you? please come in." said Mary. 'why not be civil after all Tom is Adam's father' thought Mary.

Page 5

"It's okay Mary don't worry about it. How is Adam I've come to see Adam. I had a meeting nearby with some chemist officials it ended sooner actually I ended it quickly I gave them a good deal and so they signed the deal. Now where is Adam?"

"Tom please sit down. Adam is having a nap but its time for him to wake up. I will go and get him from the bedroom. Then I will sort you some food out. You have not eaten have you?"

"No I haven't not yet, some food would be nice, thanks. I'll sit myself down in the living room.

Excited Mary walked into the bedroom and saw Adam is awake. She smiled and grabbed him into her arms, 'Hello Adam my darling, we have a guest downstairs and you probably hungry. So lets go down.' Mary and Adam happily went downstairs.

Page 6

Tom looked at his son Adam and smiled, 'Hello little tiger. Dad is here.' Tom said and opened his arms towards his son. Adam was excited to see his father. Adam happily went into Tom's arms from Mary's arms. Mary walked to the kitchen and warmed some food for Tom. After 5 minutes she came with a plate full of warm vegetable curry and basmati rice with a fork.

"That smells good." Said Tom as Mary put the plate in front of Tom on the coffee table and said, "Here pass me little Adam and you eat. Adam is happy to see you. I know you are really busy Tom but you should come over a bit more to see Adam. He is growing fast you know."

Page 7

"Mary you're right but at the moment I am busy with few new businesses the company I work for and own most of it is expanding but I will try my best I will. Look I'm here now." Explained Tom and he picked the plate of food up with the fork and began to eat. Adam is just staring at his father who he hardly sees. Tom smiled at Adam and Adam smiled back.

"He is 9 months now, is that right?" asked Tom. As he is hungry he already finished eating half the food on the plate.

Page 8

"No he is 10 months old now Tom. Erm, let me get you some water, 2 sec." Mary said and got up from the chair with Adam walked to the Kitchen and came back with a mug of cold tap water. She placed the mug of water infornt of Tom. He picked it up and drank most of it as he burped and then he finished eating. The plate is empty now and so is the mug. He put the plate and the mug down on the coffee table and said,

"Thank you for that Mary. So what else, any news any gossip. Abdullah, Mrs Rehman, is helping you with stuff right yeh, Abdullah is such a good friend and I am neglecting him as well, how is he doing and? Adam is 10 months old, wow, time goes quick!" said Tom. He looked at his Rolex wristwatch the time is 8:34pm. Mary noticed Tom looked at his Rolex.

Page 9

"Do you have to go now?" said Mary.

"Not yet, here pass me Adam let me hold my son in my arms for a bit." Said Tom. Mary was delighted to pass Adam to his father.

"About Abdullah he is fine and so are his parents. I want to tell you something Tom when you left me as you did I was angry, upset and hated you but as time passed the hate went away and yes thank you for all the money." Mary said. 'she can't believe she said that' her heart is eventually free she does not hate Tom or anyone else. There is no hatred inside her.

Is that because she has fallen in love with Abdullah? but then once upon a time she did fall in love with Tom and they got married and they got a son and now they are getting a divorce. So it must be something else. Something about the Malcolm-x story. She can't quite figure it out. How did Malcolm X overcome the hatred from the (white) people in the USA?

Page 10

"You don't hate me no more that is good we can be civil now and also Mary you are a good person. Money is no problem. If you need more just ask." Tom said as he kissed his son Adam on the left and right cheeks. That made Mary smile.

"Tell me about Abdullah and you how did you guys become friends?"
"oh yes. When we are in primary school. I was getting bullied by some older boys Abdullah comes to my rescue amazing. Afterwards I became his friend, we became friends we are best friends. He is a good friend." Said Tom. Adam is just staring at his father Tom and smiling.

"look there is something new I have to tell you but before I do you have to promise me you can't get mad at me or get mad at Abdullah." Mary said and wondered is it a good time to tell Tom? Is it to soon?

Page 11

"I won't be mad I promise what is the matter is everything okay? You've met someone?" Tom tried to guess.

"Yes I have in fact I am in love with your best friend Abdullah?" Mary said it. She couldn't keep it to her self. She decided Tom had to know and now he does.

"Wow you love Abdullah, does he know?" asked Tom. 'This is interesting and unexpected, a little surprising,' thought Tom.

"He does know, all this happened just recently. This love thing is mysterious, you love someone then you don't then you love someone else. Also I am really thinking of becoming a Muslim?" said Mary. Waiting for Tom's reaction. A man she loved once. Loved in the past.

Page 12

"I have to say Mary I am a little surprised and happy for you also. Now Abdullah is a good man and he is my best friend so that is good you two love each other now and about becoming a Muslim that is your personal thing again I have no problems with muslims. most of them are very good and one of them is my best friend." Tom said. Adam fell asleep on Tom's laps. Mary picked him up from Tom's laps and lied him down on the sofa next to Tom.

"So you are cool with all this and by the way when are you Marrying Jennifer?" Mary asked.

"Wow, normally you are mad thinking of her and now you just mentioned her name. You really have changed Mary." Tom had to ask.

Page 13

"look like you said lets be civil about all this at least for Adam's sake and also for our sake. I get it now you don't love me no more, I get it now am just being civil." Mary said. She also wanted to say 'I don't love you anymore Tom' but she did not wanted to hurt his feelings.

"Well about 5 or 6 weeks our divorce will be finalised then me and jenneifer will fix a wedding date. What about you and Abdullah?" asked Tom. He looked at his wristwatch the time is 9:16pm.

"Well Abdullah needs to talk to his parents about us after that, probably 2 months time I guess." Said Mary.

"Okay Mary that's great and Abdullah would make a good husband I am happy for you both, however I am sorry but I have to go but I promise to talk to you and Abdullah on the phone more often, okay bye." Tom said. He got up and walked to the door let himself out got into his new BMW and drove off. Mary did not had a chance to say 'goodbye' but that's Tom for you. He leaves without warning.

At home Abdullah wrote some bullet points regarding his first college assignment. He looked at the handing in date and noticed it is due on Friday so he can do it tomorrow.

In that case he walked upstairs into the bathroom to do wudu (ablution) cleansing parts of the body before ishaa salaah (Namaz). 'worshipping the Creator (Allah) is the least we can do this is because it is The Creator (Allah) who created us and everything else, the entire existence.' This Abdullah understood very well.

Page 15

Chapter 2

After doing wudu he walked into his bedroom, and placed his red and green velvety Islamic prayer mat on the clean part of his bedroom (the right corner) which he does every-day five times a day in order to read salaah facing the Qibla (Kaaba in Makka, Saudia-Arabia.) then he stood up to read the ishaa salaah.

After Salaah Abdullah does these Duas: (making request / additional worship) Abdullah raised his hands up in the air keeping them together his palms facing the ceiling, so he began saying (to himself silently) as he is now sat on the Islamic prayer mat facing the Qibla (Kaaba).

Page 16

'Asthagh-firullaah Allazzee La ilahaa illah
Huwa, al Hayyul Qayyum wa athubu ilayh. Ameen'
Abdullah paused for a few seconds. He breathed in
and out then he said it in english 'Reciting this as Dua
(request) to the Creator (Allah). First of all The
Creator (Allah) loves those who ask for forgiveness
and surely the Creator (Allah) will forgive my sins.
Ameen.' He paused again for a few seconds and then
said, 'I ask forgiveness from the Creator
(ALLAH) The one who only should be worshipped
and no one else. The one (Allah) who deserves all
worship the Creator (ALLAH) and no one else. The
ever living, no beginning and no end and also the
sustainer. I repent and ask for forgiveness to The
Creator (ALLAH), Ameen.' He paused again then
said, 'Ya Allah forgive all the Muslims and guide the
non muslims (not yet Muslims) to Islam such as my
friend Tom so they also can enter paradise with us as
Muslims, Ameen. I know it's up to them ya Allah.
This is because we all have free will and dual nature
which you gave us to test us. Asthagfirullah, ameen.
Having said all this you ALLAH know best'

Page 17

Abdullah completed his Salaah and Duas for today and he is looking forward to the morning Fajr salaah. He loves worshipping the Creator (Allah) as a muslim. (He figured islam is the truth from the Creator (Allah) by reading the Quran objectively). Abdullah believes if anyone reads the Quran objectively then he or she will become a Muslim therefore save their Ruh (soul) and go to paradise.

Abdullah felt really tired so he crawled into his bed and dozed off after saying, 'Ashadu- Allah La ilaha illallahu wahdahu laa shareeka lahoo wa ash-hadu anna Muhammadan (peace be upon him) Abduhu wa Rasooluhu.

Chapter 3

8 weeks have passed so quick for Abdullah as he was busy with assignments and working at the grocery store. He is fed up of working at the grocery store and also it is time for him to talk to his parents about marrying Mary.

Importantly Mary has become a muslim few weeks ago after reading the Quran objectively. Mary said her Shahada at the local mosque infront of other muslim sisters and the women imam. (assistant imam of the local mosque). Also Tom's and Mary's divorce has been finalised (divorce absolute)

It's the December holidays or winter holidays and Abdullah handed his assignment for this week which was on why do men try to be dominant always. He figured it has to do with the ego and arrogance.

Also how society and societies have been run for the past 10.000 years which was a male dominance society. He is enjoying this psychology course but some of it is atheistic which he did not like some past and present psychologists don't believe in the Ruh (soul) and that motivated him to write an article about what keeps us alive. Not our healthy organs because healthy people with healthy organs die in their sleep all the time. So the important question is it is not our organs that keeps us alive. Also a heart attack, stroke, cancer these cause of deaths appear to be the cause of deaths but not actually. What keeps us alive is the Ruh (soul) Abdullah figured this out and wrote an article about it and it is published on Amazon.com (What keeps us alive? By Abdullah) when the Ruh (soul) is reclaimed by The Creator (Allah) this is when we experience death. Only our earthly body dies meaning stops to function.

Page 20

Chapter 4

Abdullah voluntarily got more assignments from his teacher. Also a book on Sigmund freud and shrodinger et al to read over the weekend. He also has applied for a job at Mcdonalds, sandbrook park Rochdale.

Mary wanted to take him on dates just the two of them leaving Adam with Tom past few weekends ago but Abdullah said no because it's not allowed in islam and he does not want to knowingly commit sins. Mary understood and said we will do everything that a husband and wife does in islam after our marriage (Nikah-islamic marriage). Abdullah was pleased that Mary understood. Abdullah called her earlier and told her that today evening he will talk to his parents about their future, about their marriage.

As he is walking to his car his mobile buzzed he answered it quickly as it is his best friend Tom calling.

Page 21

"Hello Buddy how are you?" said Abdullah. He has reached his car and slid into his worn brown leather driver's seat. Holding his mobile in his left hand and listening with his left ear. 'Mary has become a muslim when will Tom become a muslim? what if Tom dies tomorrow his soul is reclaimed tomorrow by The Creator (Allah)… that thought made him freeze for a few seconds. It's not the first time he had this thought.

"Hi, I am okay matey, hello, hello? Abdullah are you there?" Tom almost shouted.

"Sorry yes I am here Buddy. Go on whats up?" said Abdullah.

"Well good news for me and Jennifer we got married today at the Rochdale town hall marriage registrar office." Said Tom. He sounds really excited.

"Oh that's great. It about time. That's is good news Tom finally you got to marry the women you love. So where are you going for your honeymoon?" Abdullah asked.

"Paris. The city of romance. Anyways listen Abdullah look you are my best friend and you are struggling financially I now that and you hate working at the grocery store let me help you please with some money. I'm your friend after all this should not hurt your pride Abdullah and you know I won't tell a soul." Said Tom.

"if you insist so much my friend. I will text you my sort code and account number later on or tomorrow." Said Abdullah. He could not delay this genuine offer of help from his best friend no more and also he does not want to hurt Tom's feelings. *'when will Tom become a Muslim. I hope Tom does not die as a non-muslim then Tom will become a never-ending tragedy. The (Creator) ALLAH knows best!'*

"That's my friend good man Abdullah and yes when are you and Mary getting married?" said Tom.

"About that yes, soon. Look Tom I gotto go home and talk to my parents about this so bye for now and thanks for everything." Abdullah said and hung up. He drove straight home. The time is 3:50 when Abdullah reached home. He quickly did wudu and read Magrib salaah. After the salaah he did his usual Duas.

Then he walked downstairs and cooked himself some pasta and cheese. Abdullah also made a super coffee for himself and so with the pasta and coffee he sat in front of the TV and began to watch the BBC news.

Nothing interested so he switched the channel using the sky remote to sky one. Mission impossible 2 is on Abdullah thought he will watch it for a while.

Chapter 5

He and Tom did see the first one last year in cinema. 'you haven't seen me upset' he still remembers Tom cruise's dialogue at the end of the first mission impossible. The sound track is pretty cool too. Abdullah finished eating and as he sipped his coffee he started to enjoy the movie. He is anxious about telling his parents about marrying Mary. However before he forgot he texted his sort code and account number to his friend Tom.

Mary looked at her kitchen wall clock it is almost 7pm. Adam is having his usual nap. She thought about ringing Abdullah but then she decided it would probably be better if she calls him tomorrow regarding what his parents have said of them getting married.

She understands there is big cultural differences but his parents do come across modern or may be she is wrong. Mary decided she will have a Raspberry tea to calm her nerves down so she instantly put the kettle on filling it halfway with cold tap water. Earlier on in the morning to be specific she had a good workout at the gym. Managed to burn 800 calories. Adam was with the baby sitter.

Mary's mind drifted to her recent past and she thought to herself 'how could you love someone so much your heart hurts and you are the happiest girl in the world and then one day suddenly he says he does not love you no more and at that moment you shatter into a trillion pieces but he does not care anymore because he just leaves you are men like that I hope not, at least not all of them. then gradually I stop loving him and fall in love with someone else. How is that possible. Love is a mystery to me.

My mother and father are not getting along. It is scary after 23 years of marriage they will be divorcing each other. My alcoholic dad never recovered from his addiction and mum has had enough. I don't blame her. I hope she finds herself a better husband. Mary stopped thinking. 'What's the point what will happen will happen. She made her raspberry tea and walked to the living room to watch law and order on sky one. 'I am muslim now and I need to read Salaah learn how to read Quran. Abdullah will teach me eventually' that thought bought a smile to Mary's beautiful face.

Abdullah knows his parents will not understand easily why he chose to marry Mary obviously because he loves her and also she loves him back. And to top it up she has become a muslim, thanks to The Creator (Allah). However today he will try to convince and persuade his parents of his choice.

chapter 6

After an hour his mother came home and after another 30 minutes his father came home. Abdullah is ready to tell them today that he has made a decision to marry Mary.

After a few minutes his parents came and sat near him on the living room chairs. Opposite him. Facing him. Smiling at him.

"So how is your course going?" asked his father happily.

"Its good, the assignments can be a bit tricky but then there is the one to one tutor support from college. Okay mom and dad I have something important to tell you." Abdullah said nervously.

"What is it? his mother asked. "whats the matter son. You look worried?" his father said.

"I don't know how to say this but here it is. I have made the decision to marry Mary." Abdullah said it. he finally said it. he has been rehearsing this for the past two hours in his mind.

"You want to marry Mary Tom's divorced wife why?" his father asked. A little angry. His mother got a little confused.

"What about Zainab?" his mother asked.

"We have already told her family you agreed to marry her after your studies which you agreed." His father said.

Chapter 7

"Yes I did dad but that was because I needed some time to think but now I have thought about all this regarding who I should marry and I have decided to marry Mary because I love her." Abdullah half heartedly tried to explain but his parents were having none of it.

"You want to marry that English girl, that new muslim girl, divorced with a child. Abdullah my son you have gone mad." His father said angrily.

"But dad I love her." Said Abdullah. A little scared. He has not seen his dad so angry before.

"We don't care if you love her or not you are going to marry Zainab the one we chose for you and that's that, Abdullah." His mother said angrily. She too is very angry regarding his decision. Abdullah did not wanted to get angry with his parents but his decision to marry Mary is final so he got up from the sofa in their living room and spoke, " mother and father I will always respect you and love you but right now I have to leave this house. I am really sorry about this. Please forgive me." Abdullah said calmly. He walked out of his home as tears filled his eyes. His parents were silent but angry and did not stop him.

They just did not believe what has happened what just took place. Their son Abdullah is leaving home. They never dreamt of this but this has happened. Abdullah is gone.

Abdullah checked his mobile for the time. It is 8:46pm. He arrived at Mary's front door and knocked on it with his right fist. He waited for almost a minute and knocked again. After a few seconds Mary opened the door. When Abdullah saw Mary his tears came rolling down his cheeks. He was a little nervous about this unusual situation which he did not expect.

"Come in Abdullah. What happened sorry I was in the bathroom that's why I couldn't get to the door sooner. Why are you crying?" Mary said worriedly and she is concerned. Adam had his evening food and now is asleep. Abdullah walked pass Mary into her living room and sat on her sofa and he cried. Several seconds later. Mary asked,

"Please tell me what has happened are your parents okay? Is Tom okay? Please stop crying and tell me what has happened? You are getting me really worried?". It took Abdullah a few minutes to regain his emotional balance.

Page 32

"My parents are fine and so is Tom. I told my mother
and father about us, about me and you getting married
and they did not approve, they want me to have an
arrange marriage. I said I can't do that and walked out
of their house, my home. What am I going to do now
Mary?" Abdullah said.

"You live here until you figure things out I do have 2
spare bedrooms but I don't want you to ruin your
relationship with your mother and father because of
me Abdullah but they don't agree us getting married
that is unfair as well." Mary said, a little worried.
'what if Abdullah don't want to marry her' this will
break her heart again. If this happens she will not fall
in love again. Her life would be miserable' Mary
thought.

Page 33

"Mary I love you and you love me. So I think we should get married first thing tomorrow. I will ring the imam at the local mosque tomorrow he will arrange our Nikah. We will be married tomorrow properly islamically is that okay with you Mary. I can't wait any longer." Said Abdullah.

"That is fine Abdullah. You are right lets get married tomorrow but what about your parents?" asked Mary. "They will come around after a while Mary don't worry." Abdullah said. 'This is what he hopes for but The Creator (Allah) knows best. The Creator (Allah) is also the master teacher (such as master artist, master programmer, master Creator, The Sustainer, Maintainer, Cherisher Nourisher, Creator and the controller of the entire existence that exists which The Creator (Allah) created.)

Page 34

Talking about the master teacher (The Creator (Allah)
whoever seeks guidance will be guided likewise when
a student is willing to learn then the teacher is happy
to teach but when the student is ignorant, arrogant,
can't be bothered then the teacher can only try.'
Abdullah was in deep thought.

"Abdullah are you okay. Like you said your parents
will come around." Mary replied. 'I hope so' she
thought.

"Oh Mary sorry I was thinking of errm, it's ok, never
mine. Lets go to sleep. Which room am I sleeping in?"
Abdullah said. He told himself he will ring his best
friend Tom and tell him what has happened.

Page 35

"The room next to mine and Adam's. the one on the left of the landing. Would you like to eat anything Abdullah?" Mary said.

"Not really. Not at the moment." Abdullah replied. He just can't believe his parents disagreed with his decision.

Time now almost midnight. Abdullah's parents could not go to sleep because they were really angry with Abdullah. They were talking with each other as Abdullah's father said, " I can't believe our son betrayed us for an English girl, for a gori."

"me too, I can't believe my son, our son left us to marry a English girl Mary a divorcee with a child? What did he see in her?" Abdullah's mother said to his father.

Page 36

What they did not realise was they were being racist. And they forget that Mary has become a Muslim and so Abdullah is marrying a Muslim.

They should be happy about this because this is what Abdullah wants. They as parents should not be possessive. Should not see Abdullah their son as an asset, cattle. They should seek happiness in his happiness. They need to read books and become cultured.

Next day, time 10am.

Abdullah slept in one of the spare bedroom in Mary's house. He woke up 30 minutes ago and using his mobile he rang the imam of the mosque and explained everything.

The imam said for Mary and Abdullah to go to the mosque at 2pm Nikah appointment. Adam is playing in his room with cuddly soft toys, crawling and rolling over. He has had his morning milk an hour ago.

Mary walked into the living room with fresh coffee and toast. Abdullah was watching the BBC news but he turned the TV off as Mary put the silver tray infront of him. He looked at Mary and smiled as he spoke;

"I have arranged our Nikah it is at 2pm at the local mosque is that okay Mary?"

Page 38

"That is good. I will arrange for a babysitter for 2pm, for two hours for Adam. After the Nikah can we go to a Halal restaurant just the two of us." Mary asked.

"Yes of-course Mary. Finally we will get married. I am happy. Are you happy?" Abdullah asked. Mary knows he is a little sad regarding his parents but like he said they will eventually come around.

"I am very happy Abdullah, of-course I am. This is what we both want. To finally get married." Mary confirmed.

"That's good I am going to Adam's room to play with Adam are you coming?" said Abdullah.

"erm, no you go ahead I need to do some cooking and cleaning." Mary said. 'finally things are getting into place. Finally Abdullah will become my husband. Importantly the best decision I took in my life is to become a Muslim' Mary thought and reassured herself. (EF-Dawah helped me a lot) islam is perfect muslims are not.

As Abdullah walked towards the stairs to go to Adam's room his mobile buzzed. He looked at the screen it flashed 'Tom Calling' he answered it instantly, "Hey buddy how are you?" Abdullah said. As he slowly walked up the stairs.

"I'm fine mate the question is how are you doing? how you holding up? your parents will come around like you said" Tom asked and reassured.

"To tell you the truth I just want to get married and I will deal with the consequences later but I am okay, you are coming Tom, yes? the Nikah is at the local mosque." Abdullah said. He has reached the landing soon he will be playing with Adam. He loves playing with Adam.

"I am really extremely sorry Abdullah my friend I can't make it I have a really important meeting with a big client in London in the afternoon but I have given you a surprise wedding gift. Check your bank account. I have to go now sorry bye." Tom said and ended the call. 'typical of Tom. Always earning more money' Abdullah thought.

Page 41

Abdullah's mother and father heard from the neighbours that Abdullah and Mary they are getting married at 2pm at the local mosque. His parents became very sad. They were hugging each other and crying on each other's shoulder. They cried for a while then the tears stopped their eyes became dry they felt tired so they decided to sleep for a while.

The neighbours had nothing better to do so they were gossiping about Abdullah and Mary getting married. Some remarks and statements were positive such as 'at least this is some form of integration'. 'muslim people are cleaner than our lots, our lots are always in the pub drunk and fighting' 'couldn't she have found another English man to marry instead of a foreigner'. The statements are endless some positive some negative.

2pm. Abdullah and Mary got married at the local mosque by the Imam infront of many witnesses just after Zuhr namaz (prayer/worship). After their Nikah Abdullah and Mary were driven by a chauffeur in a old Rolls Royce to a restaurant called Sanam on Wilmslow road, Rusholme, Manchester. They had some delicious food such as lamb jalfrezi and tandoori chicken with rice and nan. Also they had sweet mango lassi. After the meal they were driven home. Mary and Abdullah finally got married and they are really happy. Abdullah is a little sad his parents did not come to the wedding (Nikah). He does feel a little guilty.

Page 43

Next day

Jennifer finished her special K cereal and stood up in their kitchen from the leather stool she was sitting on. She is angry with Tom and his broken promises.

"You never have any time for me Tom! You promised me you were going to take me for lunch yesterday then you call me and say you can't make it. What is going on Tom don't you not love me anymore?" Jennifer angrily said. Tom could not finish his breakfast and Jennifer started the argument. This is the third argument this week.

"I love you Jennifer you know that its just I have a busy workload I am the partner and founder of 5 companies. I am building an empire. Okay listen Saturday I promise I will take you shopping then food, then bowling and also cinema I will make it up to you I promise but I really have to go now honey, my darling. Okay bye." Tom said and he was out the front door. He ran into his 500 CLK silver Mercedes started the engine and drove off.

"I hate you Tom!" Jennifer shouted where she stood. The past few days Jennifer felt very lonely. She does have a big house and lots of expensive clothes and jewellery but what she does not have is Tom spending time with her. Spending quality time with her. Tom is very busy nowadays. He is sometimes in London or Glasgow or New york or Washington. She wonders is he having an affair?

Mary and Abdullah are really happy because they are married now. They are husband and wife now. Abdullah can't believe he has finally married Mary.

After dinner Mary took Adam upstairs as he is sleepy. Mary tucked Adam in bed and Adam fell asleep instantly. Adam was playing with Abdullah morning and afternoon inside the house and also in the garden.

Mary came downstairs and walked to the kitchen she brewed some fresh filtered coffee for her and Abdullah. Few minutes have passed the coffee is ready. Abdullah is watching law and order on sky one. Mary came with coffee and cookies. Placed them on the new marble coffee table her mother and father gave her as a wedding gift. ' it's from Italy.' Her mother said on the phone that was in the morning. It's a nice day outside.

"Thank you Mary but I tell you the crime around the world is just going up. The Law and Order drama sometimes scares me you know." Abdullah said as he smiled at his wife Mary. He is a little sad regarding his parents not approving of Mary. *'may be with time they will come around'*

"You are correct law and order sometimes scares me too, people become evil when they choose to live their lives arrogantly and ignorantly no sense of care for others." Mary said as she sat opposite facing Abdullah her husband. She feels happy marrying Abdullah. She can't believe she loves Abdullah. She use to love Tom. How is this possible you can fall in love with different people. She does not hate Tom after all Tom is Adam's father.

"Adam gone to sleep eh." Abdullah asked. 'he just loves that boy' Adam will be 13 months soon. 'that boy is growing fast', Abdullah thought. He is happy that he has married Mary eventually. *'Mary is beautiful'*

"His gone to sleep soon as he was tucked inside his soft duvet. He has been running around all day with you. look at my carpet you and Adam and the kitchen floor." Mary said. She switched the TV off with the sky remote. Some questions about islam circling in her mind.

"Oh sorry about the mess I will vacumn and clean in the morning I promise but why did you turn the TV off I was watching…

"Oh the TV yes I want to talk or ask some important questions regarding islam and about the mess in the house don't worry about it. I'll clean it up later or tomorrow." Mary said interruptingly.

"Of-course what about islam, what are your questions?" Abdullah said politely. He wondered what will she ask but it is good to ask questions about islam to clear one's doubts.

"Quran is the last, final revelation I wonder why? and what about the previous books?" Mary Questioned. She felt a little uncomfortable asking the question but Abdullah smiled at her which told her it is okay to ask questions.

"Good question and I will answer your question now by the way I learnt all this from the local Muslim teachers and also my father. So yes Quran is the final revelation why? I will answer that after but firstly islam is from the beginning…

"What do you mean Abdullah, that islam is from the beginning?" Mary said interruptingly. Which Abdullah did not mind at all. He is genuinely smiling at his beautiful wife Mary. (Alhamdulillah)

"Let me explain my darling wife Mary, (Mary smiled at the word darling)
The first prophet was Adam (peace be upon him) also the first man on planet earth. The Creator (Allah) told Adam to tell his children that is also us, includes us, to worship The Creator (Allah) and to listen to Adam for the daily living stuff example how to be nice to others, sharing and caring, no stealing etc. now The Creator (Allah) told all the messengers and prophets that came after Adam the same message which is La ilaha illal lah meaning there is none worthy of worship except (The Creator) Allah." Abdullah said and he drank some good coffee. He loves coffee.

"So from Adam to Noah, I mean Nuh, ibrahim, moses, I mean musa peace be upon them all they were given the same message which is La ilaha illal lah meaning there is none worthy of worship except (The Creator) Allah." Mary said as she reassured herself.

"Yes and also the prophets being like teachers told their people how to go about daily life but importantly the message had to stay the same meaning accurate, La ilaha illal lah, so when Musa (peace be upon him) was given the message he went to his people and told them La ilaha illal lah meaning there is none worthy of worship except (The Creator) Allah. And he Musa (peace be upon him) is the messenger of Allah, that's in the past. That make sense Mary?" Abdullah said as he drank more coffee. He loves coffee.

"Yes it does and I think I figured it out so from Adam then Idris, Nuh, Hud, Salih, ibrahim, ismail, ishaq, Lut, yaqub and sorry I forgot (peace be upon them all) the other names of the prophets and messengers and of-course final prophet and messenger Muhammad (sallallahu alaihi wa sallam) was given the Quran because the previous books, revelations were tampered with." Mary said as she drank some coffee. She likes coffee because Abdullah likes coffee. She usually drinks green tea.

"That's right the previous books revelations were interfered with opinions added etc, changed by their followers and so forth but the Quran is unique it was first memorized then it was written down and since it was written down its exactly the same 114…

"114 Surahs yes I know that." Mary said happily as she interrupted.

Page 52

"So to summarise what we have been talking about is that islam is from the beginning and not when the Quran was revealed. You see it is us, the children of Adam and Hawwa (Eve) messed it all up from the beginning by adding our, people of the past I mean, opinions to the previous revelations but importantly Quran is unique and has been memorized by so many muslims all over the world. To understand the Quran one should be an expert in Arabic language. Quran has linguistic miracles. If you search Yutube for Quran linguistic miracles then you will know, and yes Quran final revelation because the previous books were tampered with opinions added, Creator's law removed and so forth but like I said islam is from the beginning. You see all the messengers and prophets came with good news and warning the good news is worship Allah as a muslim meaning only worship Allah without associating a partner and listen to the prophet and or messenger of your time, the warning is to those who reject and deny islam which is punishment in the fire of jahannam." Abdullah happily explained. Mary nodded in agreement. She too is happy and smiling.

Page 53

"So the reason Quran being the final revelation is because the previous books were tampered with ok I got that, I will search the Youtube tomorrow look into the linguistic miracles of the Quran but I do have more questions please don't get angry at me?" said Mary. A little worried.

"Not at all I am not angry or frustratred or annoyed Mary, questions in islam are welcomed, islam is practical. So what is your next question?" Abdullah asked politely. Still genuinely smiling at his wife Mary.

"How would you erm, look I know there is Allah the Creator but…

"But how do you prove The Creator (Allah) is real?" Abdullah said.

"Yes, sorry." Said Mary.

"Don't be sorry. Let me explain. So there are multiple answers firstly there is creation which are us, trees, plants, planets, stars, animals, so there is creation and obviously there is The Creator. The Creator (Allah) is uncreated by definition see the Youtube video by Dr Zakir Naik. The Creator is uncaused for argument sake if creator 1 made creator 2 then who made creator 2? And I say creator 3? Then who made creator 3? And so it becomes never ending and the existence is never created. Someone had to create the existence and that someone is The Creator (Allah)." Abdullah explained politely.

"Okay I see your explanation is amazing Abdullah. Next question, can there be more than one Creator?" Mary asked. *'Wow he knows a lot. He is a knowledgeable Muslim and my husband.'*

"No because if there was more than one Creator then we would have seen parallel creations such as cows with 8 legs and humans with 6 arms. Other planet earths next to earth other solar systems, bigger bees and wasps. Also we would see them fighting, we don't see that therefore there is only one Creator, The Creator, Allah means the one who deserves all worship." Abdullah explained. He is enjoying this. It is satisfying to explain the purpose of life to someone, anyone. In his case he is explaining everything to his wife.

Page 56

"Next question has anyone or any prophets seen the Creator Allah?"

"Well in the Quran, Moses (peace be upon him), Musa alaihi wa sallam Wanted to see the Creator ALLAH he requested to see. However ALLAH replied its not a good idea but ALLAH said "I will show myself to the mountain opposite you and if it still stands then may be you can see me." The mountain turned to dust and moses (peace be upon him) fell unconscious to the ground. ALLAH revived moses. Moses (peace be upon him) asked for forgiveness and realized that ALLAH is more powerful than the sun and our earthly bodies will just become burn toast in front of the Creator ALLAH. This is the reason we cannot see ALLAH being inside planet earth and with our earthly bodies because the earthly body is soft and fragile.

End of book 2 (The story of Tom and Abdullah)